The Debt Detox

Cleanse Your Finances and Breathe Easy

Andrew Galowey

Copyright © [Andrew Galowey] [2024]. All rights reserved. No part of this publication may be reproduced, distributed, or transmitted in any form or by any means, including photocopying, recording, or other electronic or mechanical methods, without the prior written permission of the publisher, except in the case of brief quotations embodied in critical reviews and certain other noncommercial uses permitted by copyright law.

Table Of Contents

Introduction

Chapter 1: Flush Out The Toxins: Taking Stock and Developing Your Battle Plan

Chapter 2: The Snowball Effect: Resolving Small Debts for Momentum

Chapter 3: Avalanche Power: Using High-Interest Debt to Save Money

Chapter 4: Debt Consolidation: Simplifying Your Finances for Focus

Chapter 5: Enhancing Your Credit Immunity: Repairing and Protecting Your Financial Health

Conclusion

Introduction

Are you drowning in debt? Do you feel strangled by monthly obligations and overwhelmed with the prospect of ever obtaining financial independence? You are not alone. Millions of individuals are struggling with debt, but what if there was a way to break free and breathe easier?

Welcome to "The Debt Detox: Cleanse Your Finances and Breathe Easy." This book is your road map to financial freedom. We'll look at tried-and-true solutions like the debt snowball and avalanche approaches, assisting you in determining the best strategy for your specific circumstances. We'll look at budgeting tactics to free up additional income for aggressive repayments, as well as debt consolidation options to help you manage your finances. Finally, we will assist you in restoring your credit score, laying a solid financial foundation for a healthy future.

This book is about more than simply getting out of debt; it is about giving you the tools you need to take charge of your money and achieve long-term financial success. Let's get started on your debt relief journey and recover your financial independence!

Chapter 1: Flush Out The Toxins: Taking Stock and Developing Your Battle Plan

Debt may seem like a chronic sickness, gradually draining your finances and producing continual worry. However, just as with any sickness, the first step toward healing is a comprehensive diagnosis. In this chapter, we'll conduct a financial assessment to better understand your debt environment, develop a specific battle strategy, and provide you with the tools you need to overcome it.

Financial Autopsy: Uncovering Your Debt

The first step is to acknowledge the issue. Collect all of your financial records, including credit card bills, loan statements, and student loan documentation. List each debt, including the creditor, kind of debt (credit card, personal loan, etc.), current amount, and minimum monthly payment. Be truthful and include everything, no matter how tiny or difficult it may seem. This thorough list provides a clear view of your overall debt load.

Next, arrange your debts according to their interest rates. High-interest loans, such as credit cards, may accumulate significant charges fast, making them more costly to sustain over time. In contrast, student loans may have lower interest rates, making them less urgent to repay in full. However, the overall sum and minimum payment amounts may still be large.

Do not panic! This first evaluation is about collecting information rather than providing rapid answers. Once you have a clear understanding of your debt position, we can create a specific strategy to address it strategically.

Building your budget: freeing up cash for repayment

A well established budget is the foundation of any debt removal approach. This strategy divides your income between necessary spending, savings objectives, and, most significantly, debt payback. There are several budgeting strategies available, ranging from classic pen and paper to budgeting applications.

Begin by noting your total monthly revenue from all sources, including your salary, side hustles, and other incomes. Then, scrupulously record your spending for a month. There are two types of expenses: fixed (rent, utilities, auto payments) and variable (groceries, entertainment, meals). Analyze your spending patterns to see where you may reduce money. Perhaps it's cutting down on unneeded subscriptions, dining out less, or looking for cheaper grocery and entertainment options. Every dollar saved may be used to pay off debt.

Choosing Your Weapon: The Debt Avalanche Versus The Debt Snowball

With a clear awareness of your debt and a repayment-focused budget, it's time to decide on a debt eradication approach. There are two common methods: debt avalanche and debt snowball.

The debt avalanche favors repaying loans with the highest interest rates first. While the minimum payments are paid on all obligations, any additional funds are allocated to the loan with the highest interest rate. This technique saves you the most money in the long term since it eliminates the debt with the highest interest costs.

The debt snowball focuses on repaying the lowest obligations first, regardless of interest rate. Once a tiny obligation is fully paid off, the freed-up funds are allocated to the next lowest loan. This technique gives you a feeling of success as you swiftly pay off bills, which may be a great motivation to keep on track.

Ultimately, the ideal technique is determined by your personality and financial position. If you're driven by the prospect of making speedy improvement, the snowball approach might be great. If you're more concerned with saving money on interest costs in the long term, the avalanche approach may be a better option.

Building Your Support System
Debt reduction may be a tough task, so don't be afraid to seek help. Speak with a trustworthy friend or family member who can provide support and accountability. Consider with a credit counselor or financial expert to help you create a specific debt repayment plan. There are also several online tools and forums devoted to debt-free living, which provide helpful advice, methods, and encouragement from others on the same journey.

Remember that you are not alone in this struggle. By assessing your financial condition, creating a good budget, and selecting the best debt removal approach, you've built the framework for financial independence. The next chapters will go further into particular tools and approaches for accelerating your debt repayment path. Let's start your financial detox and feel well again!

Chapter 2: The Snowball Effect: Resolving Small Debts for Momentum

Debt may seem like an avalanche, threatening to crush you behind a pile of bills and worry. But what if we could turn the tables and harness the force of snowballs? The debt snowball approach, a popular debt removal strategy, focuses on handling your smaller bills first, generating momentum and enthusiasm as you watch them decrease.

This chapter delves further into the snowball approach, detailing how it works, its advantages and disadvantages, and how to use it successfully. Buckle up and prepare to experience the snowball effect!

Understanding the Snowball Method

The snowball method's main idea is simple: prioritize and pay off your lowest bills first, regardless of interest rate. Once a tiny obligation is completely paid off, you transfer the freed-up payment amount (minimum payment plus any additional payments) to the next lowest loan. This results in a snowball effect, as your "payment snowball" becomes larger with each debt handled, helping you to tackle larger ones more quickly.

Below is an overview of the stages involved:

- List Your Debts: Similar to Chapter 1, make a detailed list of all of your debts, including the creditor, kind of debt, current amount, and minimum payment. However, this time, rank them from smallest to biggest.

- Make the minimum payment on all of your bills to prevent late penalties and significant harm to your credit score.

- Attack the Smallest obligation: Use all of your surplus funds (beyond minimum payments) to pay down the smallest obligation on your list. This might be a shop credit card with a little amount or a personal loan taken out for a minor transaction.

- rejoice Your Victory: Once even the tiniest debt has been paid off, rejoice! This success, however little it may seem, is a big step toward financial independence.

- Roll the Snowball: Add the minimum payment you were paying on the eliminated debt to the minimum payment you are now making on the next lowest obligation on your list. This additional payment enables you to pay off the following loan quicker.

- Repeat and Conquer: Continue making minimum payments on all debts while allocating your higher payment amount (including the rolled-over amount) to the next lowest loan. Repeat steps 4-6 until you've paid off all of your debts.

Benefits of the Snowball Method:
There are numerous convincing reasons why the snowball technique appeals to many individuals battling with debt. Here are some of its main advantages:

- Psychological Boost: Seeing debts go fast gives you a great feeling of success and inspiration. This is particularly useful for those who are easily discouraged by high debt amounts.

The snowball approach is simple and easy to implement, unlike the avalanche method, which requires sophisticated computations. It's simple to learn and use, making it ideal for novices.

- Increased income Flow: As you pay off modest obligations, you free up more income that was previously used to make minimum payments. This increased income flow may be folded into the snowball, hastening your debt repayment process.

- Focus on Progress: Debt eradication might be a marathon rather than a sprint. The snowball technique promotes tiny triumphs, which keeps you interested and focused on your progress.

Drawbacks To Consider

While the snowball approach has many benefits, it's crucial to be aware of its possible drawbacks:

- Potentially Higher Interest Costs: Because interest rates are not prioritized, you may wind up paying more in interest over time than with the avalanche technique, which prioritizes high-interest obligations.

- It May Take Longer: Depending on the amount of little obligations you have, being entirely debt-free may take longer than using the avalanche technique.

Make the Snowball Method Work for You
Here are some pointers to help you succeed with the snowball method:

- Visually monitor your progress by checking off paid-off bills on your list or utilizing a debt snowball tracker app. Seeing your improvement may be quite motivating.

- Find Extra Money: Look for methods to supplement your income by starting a side job or selling unneeded stuff. Even little amounts of additional income might help you pay off your debts faster.

- Avoid New Debt: While paying off current debt, fight the urge to incur new debt. This might stall your progress and extend your travel.

- rejoice Milestones: Don't simply rejoice when a debt is totally paid off; also recognize minor milestones, such as reaching halfway on a certain loan. This helps to sustain momentum.

The snowball approach is an effective instrument for paying off debt and obtaining financial independence. Understanding the pros and downsides,

Chapter 3: Avalanche Power: Using High-Interest Debt to Save Money

Debt might seem like an unstoppable landslide, threatening to crush you behind a pile of interest charges. What if we could fight fire with fire? The debt avalanche strategy addresses this issue front on, prioritizing loans with the highest interest rates first. This chapter delves into the avalanche approach, discussing its basic concepts, possible advantages and limitations, and how to use it successfully to save money on interest in the long term.

Understanding The Avalanche Method

The avalanche technique is a quantitative approach to debt eradication. The main premise is to prioritize and pay off debts with the highest Annual Percentage Rate (APR) first, regardless of balance size. Eliminating these high-interest obligations initially dramatically reduces the amount of interest you incur over time, resulting in long-term savings.

Let us go down the steps involved:

- List Your bills: Similar to the snowball technique, make a detailed list of all your bills, including the creditor, kind of debt, current amount, minimum payment, and, most crucially, the APR. Order your list from highest to lowest APR.

- Make the minimum payment on all of your bills to prevent late penalties and significant harm to your credit score.

- Attack the Highest-Interest loan: Use all of your additional income (beyond minimum payments) to pay down the loan with the highest APR on your list.

- rejoice Your Victory: Once the highest-interest loan has been fully paid off, rejoice! Even if the debt was little, this achievement saves you a considerable amount of money in interest rates over time.

- Move on to the Next Avalanche: Add the minimum payment you were paying on the eliminated debt to the minimum payment you are presently making on the debt with the highest APR on your list. This additional payment enables you to pay off the following high-interest loan quicker.

- Repeat and Conquer: Continue making minimum payments on all other debts while allocating your higher payment amount (including the rolled-over amount) to the next highest APR loan. Repeat steps 4-6 until you've paid off all of your debts.

Benefits of the Avalanche Method:
The avalanche approach provides numerous significant benefits for consumers looking to save money on interest charges:

- Saves Money on Interest: Prioritizing high-interest obligations first reduces the total amount of interest you pay throughout the life of your loan. This may save you a lot of money, particularly if you have many high-interest credit card loans.

- Strategic Approach: The avalanche technique emphasizes the "cost" of your debt, making it a more quantitative and strategic approach to debt reduction.

- Potential for quicker Payoff: Because you're reducing the obligations that accrue interest the quickest, the avalanche technique may result in a quicker total debt repayment than the snowball method.

Drawbacks To Consider

While the avalanche approach provides major financial benefits, it's crucial to be aware of its possible drawbacks:

- Less Psychological Boost: Seeing lesser debts go fast, as with the snowball technique, may be a powerful motivation. Focusing on high-interest bills first may not give the same instant feeling of success, sometimes leading to despair.

- The avalanche approach might be more difficult to apply since it includes calculations and monitoring APRs. This may need more discipline and financial expertise than the simpler snowball strategy.

- It May Take Longer to See Progress: Depending on the magnitude of your high-interest loans, it may take longer to pay them off than erasing lesser debts using the snowball technique.

Make the Avalanche Method Work for You
Here are some recommendations to help you succeed with the avalanche method:

- Automate Payments: Set up automated transfers to guarantee that minimum payments are paid on time and that any additional payments go straight toward the high-interest loan.

- Track Your Savings: Calculate the monthly interest you save by paying off high-interest bills. Seeing these figures build up may be a strong motivation to keep on track.

- Combine with the Snowball: Consider a hybrid strategy. Begin with the snowball approach to generate some momentum, then go on to the avalanche method after you've paid off a few modest loans.

- Seek Help: If the calculations and monitoring become too much, talk to a financial professional who can help you design a tailored avalanche strategy.

The avalanche approach is an effective strategy for reducing interest payments and gaining financial independence. By knowing its advantages and downsides, and adopting the advice above, you may harness its strategic approach to overcome high-interest debt and emerge

Chapter 4: Debt Consolidation: Simplifying Your Finances for Focus

Juggling various loans with varying due dates, interest rates, and minimum payments may be stressful. Debt consolidation is a possible option that combines your previous obligations into a single loan. This chapter delves into the notion of debt consolidation, its many forms, possible advantages and downsides, and how to decide if it's the best option for you.

Understanding Debt Consolidation

Debt consolidation is taking out a new loan to pay off many outstanding bills. This streamlines the repayment procedure by combining many payments into a single one. There are three primary strategies for debt consolidation:

- Personal Loan: This is a frequent choice for paying off current obligations. You may get a loan from a bank, credit union, or internet lender.

Ideally, the new loan would have a lower interest rate than your existing loans, allowing you to save money over time.

- house Equity Loan or Line of Credit (HELOC): If you possess a house with equity (market value less existing mortgage), you may use it to consolidate. A home equity loan gives a flat amount, but a HELOC is similar to a credit card with a revolving line of credit. However, these solutions carry risk since your property acts as security, and failing on the loan might result in foreclosure.

- Balance Transfer Credit Card: You transfer the balances of your previous high-interest credit cards to a new card that offers a 0% introductory APR (Annual Percentage Rate) on balance transfers. While this might be a decent choice for short-term consolidation, be mindful of possible balance transfer fees and high interest rates that will apply once the promotional period expires.

Benefits of Debt Consolidation

Debt consolidation has various possible benefits:

- Simplified payback: By combining various loans into a single monthly payment, you can monitor and manage your payback process more easily. This may make it simpler to remain on schedule and avoid late fines.

- Potentially Lower Interest Rate: The idea is to get a consolidation loan with a lower interest rate than your current debt. This may save you money on interest rates in the long run, speeding up your debt repayment process.

- Improved Cash Flow: Consolidating your monthly payments may allow you to free up some cash flow. This extra money might be used to make greater payments on the combined debt or to establish an emergency fund.

- Improved Credit Score (Potential): Debt consolidation may boost your credit score in the long term by lowering your credit use ratio. On-time payments on the aggregated loan might also be beneficial.

Drawbacks To Consider

While debt consolidation may be a strong instrument, it's crucial to understand its possible drawbacks:

- Risk of Increased Debt: If you are not disciplined with your spending habits, consolidating your debt might give you a false feeling of security, causing you to incur more debt on top of the combined loan. This may exacerbate your financial condition.

- Tempted by Easy Credit: Balance transfer cards sometimes feature large credit limits, making them tempting to use and undermining the advantages of consolidation. Keep track of your expenditures and prevent amassing additional debt on the new card.

- Qualifying for a Favorable Loan: To get a consolidation loan with a reduced interest rate, you must have a decent credit score and consistent income. If your credit score is poor, you may not be eligible for a favorable loan, making consolidation worthless.

- Prepayment Penalties: Some consolidation loans have prepayment penalties, which means you may be charged a fee if you return the loan early. Consider this in your decision-making process.

Is Debt Consolidation Right For You?

Debt consolidation is not a one-size-fits-all approach. Before making a decision, consider the following factors:

- Credit Score: A strong credit score boosts your chances of being approved for a favorable consolidation loan with a reduced interest rate.

- Discipline is required for debt consolidation in order to prevent adding additional debt to the merged loan.

- Debt Types: Consolidation is particularly effective for high-interest debts such as credit cards. Secured debts (car loans, mortgages) with lower interest rates may not be suitable for consolidation.

If you decide to go forward with debt consolidation, extensively investigate several loan choices and compare interest rates and conditions before committing.

Chapter 5: Enhancing Your Credit Immunity: Repairing and Protecting Your Financial Health

Debt reduction is a tremendous achievement, but it is just the first step toward long-term financial stability. After paying off your obligations, it's crucial to improve your credit score and create good financial practices to avoid future problems. This chapter focuses on tactics for appropriate credit card usage, making on-time payments, and keeping a healthy credit utilization ratio in order to improve credit and safeguard your financial health.

Credit Score: Understanding Your Financial Fingerprint

Your credit score is a numerical representation of your creditworthiness, kind of like a financial fingerprint that lenders use to assess your eligibility for loans, credit cards, and even insurance premiums. A strong credit score (usually more than 740) provides access to cheaper interest rates, better loan conditions, and more attractive financial products.

Several variables impact your credit score, the most important of which are:

- Payment History: This accounts for the majority of your credit score. Making timely payments on all of your obligations, including credit cards, loans, and utilities, is critical to establishing and keeping a strong credit score.

- Credit Utilization Ratio: This indicator compares the amount of credit you are utilizing to your entire credit limit. Keeping your credit usage ratio below 30% displays appropriate credit card use and improves your score.

- Credit Age: The longer your credit history, the better your credit score.

- Credit Mix: Having a diverse range of credit products, such as credit cards and installment loans (mortgages, auto loans), might help your score.

Every time you apply for a loan or credit card, a "hard inquiry" is recorded on your credit report. While a few queries may not have a substantial influence on your credit score, too many might raise red flags with lenders.

Building Credit Immunity: Strategies for a Healthy Score

Now that you've removed debt, here are some important tactics for rebuilding and maintaining a high credit score:

- Responsible Credit Card Use: After paying off your debt, do not cancel all of your credit cards. Keep one or two cards open and actively utilize them for appropriate purchases, paying off the whole sum each month. This shows appropriate credit management and keeps your credit history alive.

- Become an Authorized User: If you have a friend or family member with strong credit who is willing to add you as an authorized user to their credit card account, this may help your credit score. As an approved user, you may exploit their excellent credit history to boost your own.

- Secured Credit Card (if needed): If you have a limited credit history or a low credit score, you might consider a secured credit card. This sort of card demands a security deposit, which doubles as your credit limit. Making on-time payments on a secured card might help your credit score improve over time. Once your credit score improves, you may be eligible to switch to a typical credit card that offers higher rewards and advantages.

- Monitor Your Credit Reports: It is critical to frequently check your credit reports for inaccuracies or fraudulent activities. You may get free credit reports from the three main credit agencies (Experian, Equifax, and TransUnion) once a year at https://www.annualcreditreport.com/index.action. Dispute any inaccuracies right once to ensure that your credit report correctly represents your financial status.

- Maintain Low Credit Utilization: Don't max out your credit cards. Aim to maintain your credit utilization percentage under 30%. Pay off your credit card bills on a regular basis to keep a decent usage ratio and a high credit score.

Healthy Habits for Long-term Financial Wellness

Building a solid credit score extends beyond credit cards. Here are a few more behaviors to develop long-term financial wellness:

- Create a Budget and Stick to It: A realistic budget helps you to manage your income and expenditures, preventing you from overspending and incurring additional debt.

- Build an Emergency Fund: Set aside 3-6 months' worth of living costs in an emergency fund. This offers a financial safety net for unforeseen occurrences such as job loss or medical costs, reducing your reliance on credit cards.

- Automate Savings: Make automatic payments to savings or retirement accounts. This ensures you save regularly and contributes to long-term financial stability.

- Invest for the Future: Once you've established an emergency fund, look into long-term investing opportunities to increase your wealth. Consider talking to a financial adviser about individualized investing strategy.

- Credit immunity may be achieved by following these tactics for restoring your credit score and creating good financial habits. This financial resilience shields you against future debt traps and enables you to make educated financial choices that provide the groundwork for a safe and successful future.

Conclusion

Remember, paying off debt is a marathon, not a sprint. Celebrate any achievements, large or little. Every debt repaid and every dollar saved is a step closer to financial independence. Don't hesitate to seek assistance or support along the journey. Speak with a trustworthy friend, family member, or financial adviser. There are also various online forums devoted to debt-free living, which provide important support and fellowship from others on the same road.

With determination, discipline, and the skills taught in this book, you have not only eradicated debt, but also provided yourself with the information and techniques necessary to construct a safe and wealthy future. Financial freedom is more than simply being debt-free; it also means having the peace of mind and flexibility to pursue your goals and objectives.

So, what comes next? Perhaps you're saving for a dream trip, investing for the future, or beginning your own company. The options are limitless. Remember that financial independence is a lifetime endeavor, but you've made a huge step forward. Use the momentum you've earned to continue developing good financial habits, and see your financial well-being improve. Go on and achieve your financial objectives; you've got this!

www.ingramcontent.com/pod-product-compliance
Lightning Source LLC
Chambersburg PA
CBHW050249230526
45470CB00005B/2189